Idaho Wildlife

Animals & Mammals

Billy Grinslott & Kinsey Marie Books

ISBN - 9781965098929

Chipmunks are found in many areas. Chipmunks are small members of the squirrel family. They like to eat nuts and seeds. Chipmunks are most active during the day, especially at dawn and dusk. They have pouches inside of their cheeks so they can carry food. They are very friendly and will take food from your hand. Chipmunks need about 15 hours of sleep per day. The smallest chipmunk species is Tamias minimus, which is found throughout North America.

There are many squirrels in the wild. You may see a red or gray squirrel. The most popular is the gray squirrel. Squirrels are very acrobatic and can climb trees. Their favorite food is acorns. Squirrels hide their food in many small stashes and can find more than 90% of them later. Squirrels are fast and can run up a tree at 12 miles per hour. Newborn squirrels are blind, deaf, and hairless, and rely on their mother until they mature.

Ground squirrels are primarily active during the day and rest at night. They are known for their complex burrow systems with multiple entrances, providing shelter and escape routes from predators. Many ground squirrel species hibernate during the winter months, preparing for dormancy by gaining weight and storing food. They have good senses of vision, smell, and touch, and communicate using alarm calls.

Flying Squirrels don't fly like birds. They don't have wings. They have skin that is attached to their legs. When they jump from a tree, they spread their legs out and glide through the air. Most glides are 30 feet from tree to tree. But they can glide up to 150 feet.

Though the pika looks more like a mouse, it's related to the rabbit. Pikas live in colonies, with other pikas. When they sense danger, they will let out a shrill whistle to let other pikas know that there is danger. Unlike other mammals, pikas don't hibernate in the winter. Pikas are adapted to live in rocky, alpine environments at high elevations, above the tree line.

Ferrets have a strip of dark fur across their eyes that makes them look like they are wearing a mask. The black-footed ferret is the only ferret that is native to America. Black-footed ferrets were thought to be extinct twice. Black-footed ferrets are playful. Black-footed ferrets are agile climbers. Black-footed ferrets have been reintroduced to many states.

Pocket gophers are burrowing rodents and are known for their digging activities and unique adaptations for underground life. They have very sharp claws for digging. They create complex underground tunnel systems. Their fur-lined cheek pouches, or pockets, are used to store and transport food, like roots, tubers, and grasses, back to their burrows. They can turn their cheek pouches inside out for grooming purposes. Their tails are highly sensitive and act as feelers to help them navigate the dark tunnels, even when backing up.

Marmots can't see very far. They are most active during the day because of their poor eyesight. They like to come out of their dens in the morning and afternoon. Marmots have rough fur, small ears, and short tails. Their strong feet and claws are built for digging holes in the dirt. They are nicknamed the whistle pig, for the high-pitched chirp they make to warn other group members of potential Danger.

There are many types of rabbits in the wild. The most common is the cottontail. Rabbits are cute, friendly, and fun to watch. Many people have rabbits for pets. They have soft fluffy fur. They are called cottontails because they have a white fluffy tail that looks like a cotton ball.

The hare is bigger than a rabbit with longer ears and legs. Their longs legs help them to run fast. They are agile and faster than most rabbits. Hares have excellent hearing and vision. Hares have large ears and eyes that are positioned on the sides of their head, giving them a wide field of vision. Hares can change color. Hares have the ability to change color depending on the season and their surroundings.

Pee-ewe what is that stinky critter with the big bushy tail. It smells bad. Skunks are normally curious and friendly unless you scare them. If you scare them, they will flip their bushy tale at you and spray you with a smelly potion and it stinks. Skunks spray a smelly, sulfur-based liquid from their anal glands as a defense mechanism. The spray can cause eye irritation and temporary blindness. Skunks are highly adaptable and can thrive in many different environments. Skunks have strong forefeet and long claws for digging. Skunks live in dens.

Raccoons like to come out at night. Their eyes are made so they can see in the dark. Raccoons are highly intelligent and can solve problems. They can learn to open doors, trash cans, and other containers. They are called masked bandits because they like to raid and eat out of trash cans at night. Raccoons can survive in many environments.

Ringtails look like a racoon. They have stripes on their tails, but their face more resembles a cat. They are a member of the racoon family. Ringtails can be found in some parts of North America. Ringtails are excellent climbers capable of ascending vertical walls, trees, rocky cliffs and even cactus. They are mostly nocturnal. Ringtails are agile climbers and leapers, with hind legs that can rotate 180 degrees. Their long tails help with balance. Ringtails have anal glands that produce a foul-smelling secretion.

Beavers use their teeth to cut and knock down trees. They build dams with them to block water, so they have a place to live and swim. They also eat wood. Beavers can stay underwater for about 8 minutes. Beavers slap their tails on the water to indicate danger. Beavers are the largest rodents in North America.

Otters have the thickest fur of any animal. The otter is one of the few mammals that use tools, like rocks to break thing open. A group of otters resting together is called a raft.

Otters primarily rely on their sense of touch, whiskers, and forepaws, in murky waters to locate food. Otters have built in pouches of loose skin under their forearms to stash extra food when diving.

Badgers have elongated heads, small ears, and black and white faces. Badgers live underground with other family members. Badgers are very social and live in groups. A badger den or sett can be centuries old and are used by many generations of badgers. Badgers are very territorial, it's best not to bother them is you see one. A group of badgers is called a cete, though they are often called clans. Badgers are largely nocturnal but reduce their activity during periods of cold weather.

The American Mink lives across most of North America and is a cat sized. Mink are very skilled climbers and swimmers. They prefer to keep to themselves. They communicate using odors, visual signals, and other sounds. They purr when they're happy. Mink are agile swimmers, and they often dive to find food

Martens live in a variety of habitats, including forests, woodlands, and snowy areas. Martens can be distinguished from fishers, because martens are smaller, have orange on their throats and chests, and have pointier ears and snouts. Martens are part of the weasel family. They are very rare and hard to find. Their tail is long, about two thirds of their body size. There are 13 subspecies of American marten that are native to North America.

Weasels are the smallest members of the meat-eating animals. Although small, they do not hibernate and are active all winter. Weasels in northern ranges turn white in the winter to camouflage in the snow. Weasels have long whiskers like cats, to help them feel things. They even have long whiskers on their elbows. When a weasel gets annoyed, it stomps its feet, just like humans do. Weasels are quick, agile, and alert animals. They are excellent climbers and swimmers.

Wolverines are 30–50 inches long, with a tail of 7–10 inches. They weigh 25–60 pounds. A wolverine's color patterns are unique. No wolverine has the same fur color as another. Wolverines don't hibernate in the winter. They sleep in caves, rock crevices, or under fallen trees. Wolverines have a keen sense of smell that can detect another animal 20 feet under the snow. Wolverines have poor eyesight and are active at night. Wolverine babies are called kits. They are born with white fur that turns brown as they age.

Mallard ducks are by far the most recognizable and popular ducks in the world. They live in just about every area of North America. Their estimated population is around 19 million birds. The male is easily recognizable from its white neck ring and green neck and head. The female Mallard has between five to 14 light green eggs. Most ducks don't have green eggs, so this makes them unique. The male Mallard is called a drake and the female a hen. Female Mallards quack. Males don't quack, instead they produce deeper, raspier one- and two-note calls. They can also make rattling sounds by rubbing their bills against their flight feathers.

Canada Geese are the most sought after and abundant goose in North America. They live in many places. Canada geese can travel 1,500 miles in a day if the weather permits. Canada geese migrate every year. They fly in a V-formation, which allows them to travel long distances without stopping, as they can switch positions and conserve energy. Canada geese are known for their distinctive honk and are sometimes called Canadian honkers.

Ringed Neck Pheasants are one of the most sought-after birds in North America. They are found throughout most of Northern America and Canada. Ring-necked pheasants are not native to the US. Instead, they were brought here from Asia in the 1880's. South Dakota is one of the best places to find Pheasants.

The Wild Turkey is a large, bird that is native to North America. It is the heaviest bird in the United States and can weigh up to 24 pounds. Only male turkey's gobble. Wild turkeys can fly. Wild turkeys sleep in trees. Their heads can change colors. You can tell a turkey's emotions by the color of their heads. Colors can change from red to blue to white, depending on how excited or calm they are. You can find wild turkeys in just about every state in America.

Idahois home to several types of grouse, including sage grouse, dusky grouse, also known as blue grouse, ruffed grouse, and sharp-tailed grouse. Grouse, particularly ruffed grouse, are interesting birds known for their unique drumming displays. They flap or rotate their wings, and it sounds like drums. Grouse range in size from the small white-tailed ptarmigan at 13 inches long to the sage grouse at 30 inches long.

Bald eagles are large birds, with females up to 43 inches long and weighing up to 13 pounds. Their wingspan can be up to 7 feet wide. Bald eagles build the largest nests of any bird, up to 13 feet wide and weighing more than half a ton. Bald eagles aren't actually bald. The name bald eagle comes from the old English word piebald bird, which meant white-headed bird. Bald eagles have the best eyesight of any bird. A bald eagle can see up to three miles away, which is about four to five times farther than a human. They can also see small details like an ant on the ground from great distances.

Bobcats are named for their short, bobbed tails with white tips. They have similar markings to lynxes but are much smaller. Bobcats live in a variety of habitats. Bobcats are skilled at leaping and can run up to 30 miles per hour.

The Lynx is larger than the bobcat and has lighter fur and more spots. The lynx is more than twice the size of a house cat. Lynx have natural snowshoes for feet because they have long hair on their feet. Lynx like to hunt at night. They have excellent hearing and eyesight, and can spot a mouse from 250 feet away. Lynx have colors that help them blend into their surroundings. Each lynx has a different pattern, similar to a human fingerprint.

The cougar has a number of different names, it's also known as the mountain lion. They are the fourth largest cat in the world. The cougar has the largest range of any wild cat in the North America. A cougar can jump upward 18 feet from a sitting position. They can leap up to 30 feet horizontally. Cougars cannot roar like a lion, but they can make calls like a human scream.

The Kit or swift foxes are native to much of the western United States and northern Mexico. Kit foxes are the smallest foxes in North America, weighing only about five pounds.. Despite their slender size, they have large ears to help aid their hearing and to dissipate heat. Kit foxes are mainly active at night and resting in their dens during the day. kit foxes can survive without fresh water, by getting all their fluids from their food.

There are both red and gray foxes. Red foxes have excellent hearing, allowing them to hear rodents digging underground from miles away. When afraid, red foxes grin or look like they are smiling. Red foxes front paws have five toes, while their hind feet only have four. Foxes dig underground dens where they raise their kits and hide from predators. A group of foxes is called a skulk or a leash. Babys are called kits and females are called vixens.

The coyote is bigger than a fox weighing between 20 and 45 pounds. Eastern coyotes are part wolf. Coyotes are great for pest control. They like to eat mice and rats. They can adapt and live almost anywhere, even in the city. Coyotes are very smart and have been observed learning and following traffic signals in some cities. They have a yip type of call when they communicate with each other. Coyotes are found in all the United States, except Hawaii.

Wolves, coyotes, and foxes are all part of the dog family. The Great Plains wolf, also known as the gray wolf, is the largest wolf in North America. Wolves are legendary because of their spine-tingling howl, which they use to communicate. Each wolf has its own unique howl. Wolves are born deaf and blind, but their senses develop at about two weeks. They like to roam in packs of 2 to 25 wolves. Their territory size is 25 to 150 square miles. You can see gray and red wolves in many areas of North America.

Black bears are the smallest members of the bear family in North America. Black Bears love to eat sweet things like berries, fruits, and vegetables. They are good climbers and fast runners. They are excellent swimmers and can paddle at least a mile and a half in freshwater. They usually sleep for long periods of time and hibernate during the winter. They typically try to stay away from people unless they find food in the area.

Brown bears are often called Grizzly bears, but they're not. Brown bears can grow to seven feet tall. Brown bears eat mostly grass, roots, and berries but will eat fish and other small mammals. They are commonly silent but can communicate with grunts, roars, or squeals.

Grizzly bears are a subspecies of the brown bear. They are called Grizzly bears because they have silver tips on their hair, a grizzled look. The hump on a Grizzly bear's back is a huge muscle. Grizzly bears don't hibernate like other bears. They are highly intelligent, have excellent memories and great smell. They are good swimmers and fast runners.

There are several types of antelopes, this one is known as the pronghorn. Antelopes have extremely developed senses which help them detect danger. They are quick runners and can run up to 60 mph. They can maintain high speeds for longer periods of time than cheetahs. They all like to live in herds. Antelopes don't outrun other animals. They out maneuver them. They can twist and turn very quickly. They are related to cows, sheep, and goats.

The whitetail deer is the most popular deer in North America. Whitetail deer have good eyesight and hearing. They can detect small sounds from a quarter of a mile away. Only male deer grow antlers, which are shed each year. Whitetail deer are good swimmers and will use large streams and lakes to escape predators. A young deer is called a fawn, a male is a buck, and a female is called a doe. They are the most common deer species and live everywhere in North America.

Mule deer get their name because of their mule like ears. Male deer are called bucks and females are does. Males grow new antlers every year. They can run 45 miles per hour. Mule deer can jump 2 feet high and up to 15 feet in distance. They are bigger than whitetail deer and prefer living in the mountain areas. A mule deer's eyes are located on the side of its head, providing 310 degrees of vision. Mule deer have great night vision.

Mountain goats can jump 12 feet in one leap. They like to live in high altitude environments. A mountain goats fur coat has a double layer that sheds in the summer and provides warmth in the winter. They have hooves designed to grip onto rocks to keep from falling. Both male and female mountain goats have horns. You can tell a mountain goat's age by counting the rings on its horns.

The bighorn sheep is part of the sheep family and likes to live in mountainous areas. Females are called ewes and males are called rams. They are called rams because they like to use their horns to slam into things. Their horn size is a symbol of how high they rank in the herd. The bigger their horns are, the higher they rank. Their large curled horns that can weigh up to 30 pounds. Bighorn sheep are excellent climbers and can stand on ledges as narrow as 2 inches.

Elk are the second largest members of the deer family. Bulls can weigh up to 1,100 lbs. Elk antlers can grow up to an inch per day. They can run 40 miles per hour and outrun horses. Elk have a good sense of hearing and can swivel their ears back and forth. Elk have eyes on the sides of their heads and can see in every direction except directly in front or behind. They make a cool bugling sound when communicating with other elk. It's fun to listen to them.

Wild horses, also known as mustangs, roam free in Idaho on public lands managed by the Bureau of Land Management. These horses are descendants of domestic horses released or that escaped into the wild. The BLM manages six Herd Management Areas in Idaho, with a total of around 762 wild horses on approximately 418,000 acres. Wild horses come in a variety of colors and coat patterns. Wild horses are a symbol of the American West and are seen as a part of the natural ecosystem of public lands.

There are six different subspecies of moose. Moose are built for cold areas and like living in cold regions with snow. Moose are the largest members of the deer family. Moose are huge and weigh up to 1500 pounds. Moose love water and are good swimmers. Moose have poor eyesight but compensate with a good sense of smell and hearing. At 5 days old they can outrun a person.

The North American Bison and Buffalo are sometimes confused as the same animal, but they are not. Bison have long hair on their backs, front, and a long beard. Bison are bigger than buffalo. They are the largest mammal in North America and weigh up to 2,000 pounds. Bison can run up to 35 miles per hour. They can jump 6 feet vertically and more than 7 feet horizontally. Bison calves are nicknamed red dogs, because of their orange-red color at birth.

Fun Facts about Idaho Animals

1 – Idaho does not have a state animal. They have 16 state emblems or symbols, and the State Horse is the Appaloosa.

2 - Pronghorn antelopes are the fastest land mammal in North America, capable of reaching speeds of up to 60 miles per hour.

3 - Wolverines are the largest member of the weasel family.

4 - The black-footed ferret is the only ferret species in North America.

5 - Moose are the largest members of the deer family. Moose can weigh up to 2,300 pounds and stand up to 6'11" at the shoulders.

6 - Grizzly Bears are primarily located in northern and eastern Idaho. Grizzly bears can reach top speeds of up to 40 mph.

7 - Idaho once had a large bison population, and while not as abundant now, they are still present in the state.

8 - Mountain Lions are the largest wild cat in Idaho, they are found throughout the state.

9 - Idaho is home to over 99 mammals, 230 birds, 22 reptiles, 13 amphibians, and 39 fish.

Author Page

Billy Grinslott & Kinsey Marie Books

ISBN - 9781965098929

Thanks

www.ingramcontent.com/pod-product-compliance
Lightning Source LLC
Chambersburg PA
CBHW060848270326
41934CB00002B/41